SNAPPING TURTLES

By Kathleen Conno

Please visit our website, www.garethstevens.com. For a free color catalog of all our high-quality books, call toll free 1-800-542-2595 or fax 1-877-542-2596.

Library of Congress Cataloging-in-Publication Data

Connors, Kathleen
            Snapping turtles / by Kathleen Connors.
cm. – (Really wild reptiles)
Includes bibliographical references and index.
Summary: This book tells about snapping turtles including physical characteristics, habitat, aggressive behavior, and how they raise their young.
Contents: Snap! – Common snappers – The big gator – Warming up in water – What a grump! – Nest and go – Hot or cold – The hunter – Turtle soup.
ISBN 978-1-4339-8385-6 (pbk.)
ISBN 978-1-4339-8386-3 (6-pack)
ISBN   978-1-4339-8384-9 (hard bound) –
1. Snapping turtles—Juvenile literature   [1. Snapping turtles   2. Turtles]
I. Title
                              2013
597.92/2—dc23

First Edition

Published in 2013 by
Gareth Stevens Publishing
111 East 14th Street, Suite 349
New York, NY 10003

Designer: Sarah Liddell
Editor: Kristen Rajczak

Photo credits: Cover, pp. 1, 13 Ryan M Bolton/Shutterstock.com; p. 5 dcwcreations/Shutterstock.com; p. 7 Barry Blackburn/Shutterstock.com; p. 9 Joseph T Collins/Photo Researchers/Getty Images; p. 11 Bruce MacQueen/Shutterstock.com; p. 15 Leonard Lee Rue III/Photo Researchers/Getty Images; p. 17 altrendo nature/Stockbyte/Getty Images; p. 19 Michael Woodruff/Shutterstock.com; p. 20 Tyler Fox/Shutterstock.com; p. 21 Gerald A DeBoer/Shutterstock.com.

Printed in the United States of America

CPSIA compliance information: Batch #CW13GS: For further information contact Gareth Stevens, New York, New York at 1-800-542-2595.

Contents

Snap! 4

Common Snappers 6

The Big Gator 8

Warming Up in Water 10

What a Grump! 12

Nest and Go 14

Hot or Cold 16

The Hunter 18

Turtle Soup 20

Glossary 22

For More Information 23

Index 24

Words in the glossary appear in **bold** type the first time they are used in the text.

SNAP!

Have you ever seen a snapping turtle? It's possible! They're found all over North and Central America. If you do see one, be careful! These large turtles aren't friendly.

Snapping turtles are commonly shades of black, brown, and green. They have a big head with a sharp beak. A snapping turtle's long tail and rough-looking shell make it easy to recognize. There are several **species** of this wild **reptile**, but the common snapping turtle and the alligator snapping turtle are the best known.

What a Wild Life!

In 1937, someone reported finding an alligator snapping turtle weighing more than 400 pounds (182 kg) in a Kansas river.

COMMON SNAPPERS

Common snapping turtles can be found from Canada all the way to northwestern South America. An uneven edge running down the top of their tail makes them easy to spot. It looks like a saw! They weigh about 10 to 35 pounds (4.5 to 16 kg).

A common snapping turtle's shell is about 8 to 12 inches (20 to 30 cm) long. When young, their shells have three ridges along them. These wear down by the time the snapping turtle is an adult.

A snapping turtle has a shell under its body, too. This part of the shell, called the plastron, looks like a cross.

What a Wild Life!

Unlike other kinds of turtles, snapping turtles can't draw their head or other body parts into their shell. It's too small.

THE BIG GATOR

The alligator snapping turtle is the largest freshwater turtle. The biggest of these may weigh more than 200 pounds (91 kg). It's usually about twice the size of a common snapping turtle!

Most often found in the southeastern United States, the alligator snapping turtle has a few features that make it stand out. Its top shell, or carapace, has rough ridges called keels on it. It also has its eyes on the sides of its huge head. Other snapping turtles have eyes that face forward.

Sometimes, the alligator snapping turtle is called the "dinosaur of the turtle world" because of how it looks.

What a Wild Life!

The alligator snapping turtle has a pink, wormlike part inside its mouth. It uses this to **lure** fish into its mouth!

9

WARMING UP IN WATER

Snapping turtles spend most of their life in water. From lakes to swamps, many bodies of freshwater could be home to a snapping turtle or two!

Like other reptiles, snapping turtles are cold-blooded. Their body temperature depends on their surroundings. Many turtles like to lie, or bask, in the sun to warm up. Snappers bask in their watery **habitats** instead. You might see just the top of a snapper's head and shell peeking out from under the water!

Can you spot the basking snapper?

What a Wild Life!

Snapping turtles can stay underwater for 40 to 50 minutes at a time.

WHAT A GRUMP!

Snapping turtles are known for being **aggressive**. If something bothers them, they'll raise their body up and charge at it with their sharp beak open. Common snapping turtles give off a bad-smelling odor, too. It's no wonder snapping turtles commonly live alone!

Snapping turtles are most active at night. They often spend the day in the muddy bottom of a river or lake. No matter the time of day, though, the snapping turtle is at the top of its food chain—adults face no natural **predators**.

What a Wild Life!

Snapping turtles may stay so still underwater that tiny, plantlike creatures called algae grow on their shells.

A snapping turtle's powerful bite can cause a lot of harm.

13

NEST AND GO

One of the few times you'll find a snapping turtle out of the water is when a mother lays her eggs. About 2 months after finding a **mate**, a female snapping turtle lays as many as 50 eggs. Some snappers may return to the same nesting place each time, though that may mean walking 1 mile (1.6 km) or more!

Once she has laid her eggs, a mother snapping turtle's job is done. She covers the nest and heads back to the water.

Mother snapping turtles use the claws on their feet to dig nests. They like moist soil and sunny spots, and often choose places that are slightly raised.

What a Wild Life!

In some areas, snapping turtles like to lay their eggs in people's gardens!

HOT OR COLD

The eggs in a snapping turtle nest are small, soft, and white. They look a lot like ping-pong balls! Snapping turtles usually hatch in the late summer or fall. The babies look like tiny copies of their parents.

An egg's temperature causes the baby turtle growing inside it to be male or female. Medium temperatures produce male turtles. If the egg is a colder or warmer temperature, the egg will be female. That's pretty wild!

What a Wild Life!
Snapping turtle eggs and babies are a tasty meal for raccoons, fish, and birds.

Baby snappers will soon find their way to the nearest body of water—if they aren't eaten first.

THE HUNTER

With its strong bite and aggressive nature, the snapping turtle is a scary predator. However, one common way snapping turtles hunt is fairly calm—unless you're the **prey**!

A snapping turtle's body blends in with the bottom of a body of water. It often covers itself with mud, too. Then, it waits for a fish to swim by. Snap! The turtle traps the fish in its mouth and swallows it whole or chomps it in half with its beak.

Snapping turtles eat frogs, snakes, plants, and even other turtles!

What a Wild Life!

Snapping turtles that live in places with cold winters may **hibernate**. They dig into the mud on the bottom of shallow streams and lakes or lay in holes dug by other animals.

19

TURTLE SOUP

Snapping turtles don't have anything to fear from other animals in their habitats. Humans are their main predator. People have been hunting and eating snappers—and their eggs—for a long time. In fact, many restaurants in the United States have snapper on their menu!

Some kinds of snapping turtles are in danger of dying out, though. Some states have passed laws limiting the hunting of snapping turtles. Even if you love turtle soup, we need to keep these big reptiles around!

Super Snappers!

carapace

beak

tail

plastron

claws

GLOSSARY

aggressive: showing a readiness to attack

habitat: the natural place where an animal or plant lives

hibernate: to be in a sleeplike state for an extended period of time, usually during winter

lure: to bring an animal closer

mate: one of two animals that comes together to produce babies

predator: an animal that hunts other animals for food

prey: an animal that is hunted by other animals for food

reptile: an animal covered with scales or plates that breathes air, has a backbone, and lays eggs, such as a turtle, snake, lizard, or crocodile

species: a group of plants or animals that are all of the same kind

FOR MORE INFORMATION

Books

Bredeson, Carmen. *Fun Facts About Turtles!* Berkeley Heights, NJ: Enslow Publishers, 2008.

Hibbert, Clare. *The Life of a Turtle.* Chicago, IL: Raintree, 2005.

Websites

Snapping Turtle
www.biokids.umich.edu/critters/Chelydra_serpentina/
Find out more about snapping turtles.

Snapping Turtle Information for Kids
www.ehow.com/about_6375920_snapping-turtle-information-kids.html
Read fun facts about snapping turtles.

INDEX

alligator snapping turtle 4, 5, 8, 9

babies 16, 17

beak 4, 12, 18, 21

Canada 6

carapace 8, 21

Central America 4

claws 15, 21

common snapping turtle 4, 6, 8, 12

eggs 14, 15, 16, 20

eyes 8

habitat 10, 20

hibernate 19

humans 20

jaws 5

keels 8

lure 9

mother 14, 15

nest 14, 15, 16

North America 4

odor 12

plastron 7, 21

prey 18, 19

ridges 6, 8

shell 4, 6, 7, 8, 10, 12

South America 6

species 4

tail 4, 6, 21

United States 8